2 A.M.

THE THOUGHTS ARE HERE TO STAY

RAAHI

To everyone who made me feel so much.

Indebted forever.

Contents

Preface

My therapist tried very hard to get me to keep a diary of my thoughts and feelings. Like a stubborn little child, I always managed to avoid the task. I dread journaling so much! It's funny that people have been advising me on different ways of journaling, and even Apple didn't miss a chance to give me a 'Journal'. Do you think I started doing it after that? Not a chance!

I recently discovered why I have never listened to people's advice to write everything I feel. It's because I can't write 'anything'. I love to be poetic and dramatic with my writing and I want to express myself. I don't want my words to be trapped inside pages, so I give it all to you. You are the voice of all my unheard and unexpressed feelings.

Through this book, I am not only releasing my 2 a.m. thoughts, but also inviting you to be a part of my journey and share your feelings with me. Remember, only our expression can set us free.

So here I am, writing all my thoughts unfiltered and honestly, to free myself from all the bottled-up thoughts that never let me sleep in peace. If it resonates with you, know that we are all in this together. If not, I envy you!

Why the title '2 a.m.'? I have experienced some strange things every time I stay up late at night. The brutality I faced at 2 a.m. is beyond measure. There were nights when I wanted to kill myself because the demons that rose from their graves were far stronger than my ability to tame them. Most of my writings in this book are a piece of me bleeding ink and begging for help, writing everything as it came to me.

I believe that 2 a.m. is when we fight ourselves and our darkest emotions and memories. This is when the toughest battles are fought. The moment 3 a.m. arrives, that's the time of recovery and by 4 a.m. we are all sober and ready to face the world with a smile.

I pray to the Almighty that we all win the battles we don't talk about. We all deserve an abundant life filled with love.

Stay strong!

Acknowledgements

♥♥♥

Bhaiya, Mama, Mami, and Papa
You all have contributed to the completion of this book in many ways.
Thank you!

Prologue

Dear reader, this book is a collection of all my writings that have made me feel better. It is a testament to the struggles we all go through in our lives but choose to keep hidden from the world. I acknowledge the act and appreciate the courage to hold on to so many things and still appear unperturbed on the outside. However, I also understand the importance of opening up and letting go of all the feelings and thoughts that can hold you down.

Dear reader, if you join me on this journey of liberation, I want you to promise to be kind to yourself and to hold on to your faith until the end. The following chapters may reveal some emotions that you may not wish to explore. I advise you to take a deep breath and read on with a smile.

Sit back and enjoy the ride!

1

Love Finally Found Me

Lately, I have been wondering if love is meant for me or if I am meant for love or not. I have tried to be lovable and do what others want me to do. But the emptiness inside me won't let me be free. Hence the question of whether love is for me or not.

I am a writer and proud to be one, but reality is creeping up on me and making me admit that I was forced to choose writing. I can't talk. Building trust and sharing my scars and, as the famous cliché goes, having someone paint stars around my scars, is way beyond my reality.

I have met some wonderful people on my journey so far and I wanted them to be with me to the end. Does what you wish for ever come true? Or do you just spend your life praying for things to go your way? Either they went away or I pushed them away before they could leave me stranded with my never-ending thoughts. Yet the results have been consistent.

Rumi said, "What you seek is seeking you." Is love seeking me? If so, how long will it take for love to find me, completely shattered and destroyed by my thoughts and trapped in my mind?

I wanted to welcome love and give it a warm embrace, but the warmth in me has died and all I have is a cold breath. How can I offer this graveyard of flowers to something so beautiful that it is worth dying for?

No. I can't be there for love because it was never there for me when I needed it most. Love may seek me out, but it will never find me. Love will have to suffer the pain of separation and be devoid of affection, like me. Love will be afraid to be loved, like me. Love will be tormented and choke on the tears it holds back. And I will watch from afar with pitiful eyes.

Love will one day be on my doorstep, but I'll be gone!

2
The Spotlight

I was in Year 6 and this was the first time I had worked up the courage to enter a debating competition. I spent at least a week preparing my speech. I planned a dramatic entrance on stage, wrote some slogans, and practiced saying them out loud. I also wrote some jokes to give the audience an entertaining package. The stage was set for me to nail my first-ever stage performance. The day arrived and I was a little nervous but more excited. It was my turn and I went on stage. I was confident. But the moment I saw the audience, my confidence left me and I flew away. My legs were shaking, my throat was dry, and I still think I had a desert of lost words in my mouth. My palms were sweaty and I had all the symptoms of an anxiety attack. To add to the drama, my older brother walked into the room. He is my biggest support system, but at that moment he was the last person I expected to see. He was the rock star of the school and here I was, standing in front of at least 50 students, blank. The only thing I could say was, "My name is Shreeyank Kumar Ojha".

At least a decade has passed and I still remember that day vividly. Strangely, I am the only one who remembers it. For all the years I was in school, I avoided going on stage again because of that one day. I can relive that moment with a snap of my fingers and no one remembers. How strange and unfair is that? That fiasco changed me; my friends were in the audience and nobody seems to remember anything from that day! But the question is why?

Our successes and failures are part of our own lives. They hardly affect anyone else. Yet we spend all our time worrying about what people will think of us. Believe me, they don't. All that doubt and worry makes us more cautious in our judgment, and we tend to lose sight of what's more important: ourselves. What people think of us is just a reflection of how they see the world. The same goes for us. To turn this around, let us all start to make it a habit to always be compassionate towards others, but let us start with ourselves. The embarrassing failures or triumphant successes will go through us first, and only then will they be shared with others. Sounds a bit selfish, doesn't it? The world can take a little selfishness.

We spend most of our lives educating ourselves on a mountain of subjects. We use some of them in our lives, and we let go of many of them. But the grades will only give us a moment's satisfaction, or maybe help us get a few notable interviews. But what you take with you is the grace and wisdom you gain along the way. Most of our learning comes from experience. We learn to ride a bike mostly by falling a lot. Eventually, we learn.

When I went to college, I made it a point to put all my fiascos behind me and start again. If you are wondering if this thought had much effect, I would like to tell you that it did not. I still wondered what others thought of me, and I carried all that weight of public image for quite some time. Even though I never failed in public, opinions were very important to me. So I found out. The main problem I faced was not about performing in front of an audience. It was about failing in front of them.

So I gave myself that space to make mistakes and accepted the fact that I am no closer to being perfect and that I have my share of imperfections. But I am willing to learn and grow over time. And that, my friends, has made all the difference.

Now I am known as a good public speaker, a great stage performer and a poet who has written two books that have been loved by people of all ages. Am I still failing? Oh yes! Do I worry about what others think of me? It's not even a question now.

Now I can proudly say, "My name is Shreeyank Kumar Ojha and I have the spotlight on me and I am the rock star of my life! Just like you".

3

It's All the Same

It's all the same. I'm lying on my bed, looking at this beautiful false ceiling above me. And I wonder if that's the only 'false' thing I have in my life. I think not. Soon I will get up before everyone else. Play some really loud and happy music. I'm going to have some intense workouts and tell everyone that I had the most peaceful sleep last night. I'll jokingly compare my sleep to Kumbhakarna's. What an amazing life!

But what happens when the world is asleep?

When the dust settles and everyone finds comfort in their homes, some of us lock ourselves in our rooms and stare straight at the ceiling. I was afraid that the fan would fall down or that the roof would just collapse. Shall we run away? Darling, we just don't. We just wait for the day when it happens. Just so we can live our end without choosing it and be villains again.

We count every second of the night; we calculate when to get up and what songs to play in public to give them a "false" sunrise. We are deceitful and we play with our emotions. We are the happiest creatures you will ever see but don't you dare sneak up on us. We breed a thousand demons inside, just waiting to take over; you don't want to be a part of it.

We are the artists who stop in the middle of their work because their ability to express themselves might just unleash the beasts, with no one to tame them or love them back to life. We have a treasure trove of unfinished and directionless pieces.

If you find it divergent, know that we have just escaped something catastrophic.

But in the end, it's all the same.

4

Hope is a Curse

I talk to people and make them feel good. I see them happy and I know there's someone beyond the clouds who's happy about it. But sometimes I feel like howling at everyone and fighting every chance I get. It doesn't matter if I cry or laugh if I'm happy or sad, she never comes back, I feel her energy.

I feel her taking care of me and protecting me from people, from the world, from myself. But it's a strange world, and without her hand gently combing my head, I can't sleep.

Hope is a curse, and it will kill you, but it will never let you move on. You will always have your eyes glued to the door. "They will come back." No, they won't. They cannot!!!!

You keep waiting because someone fooled you by saying "Sabr ka fal meetha hota hai". And you keep hoping for a tighter hug, a longer conversation, and someone to feed you again. You don't sleep, you don't eat, and you don't talk. You let everything and everyone around you fade away and focus on that one thing, that one person you've lost. You try to hold on to the memories as your mind tricks you and takes them away one by one.

You don't cry because you're "hopeful". You don't accept the loss because you are 'hopeful'. But in reality, you're lost....Your life ended with them. You can't go on; you can't go back. And that treacherous hope will tear you apart, but it won't kill you. Hope will wrap itself around your neck and strangle you, but no, it won't kill you. And this curse will haunt you forever.

5
The Delusion

There's a strange story in my head about dancing. I can't tell the difference between fiction and reality, but whenever I think about it, my heart aches: it's a dilemma when the ones who saved you are the ones who ended up killing you. It's a shock! You don't know how to react, whether to trust their actions or wait until they tell you it was just a prank. And you wait and wait and wait...

Then the abuse starts, another story is woven around you, and everyone looks at you with suspicion; you're the villain again.

What people forget in all this drama is that you have your own story. But the shock takes away your ability to tell your side of the story, and the betrayers eventually win: they tell you that they care about you and love you, but you feel that they are leaving you and moving on without you. You wonder if the good times were real or just an illusion.

You start to fight the voices in your head again, and you start to lose the battles again. You find it hard to trust people again and you start to isolate yourself again. You let those suicidal thoughts win again; you let your heart break again. You see people stealing your smile again, and you see them laughing at you again, and you don't just go back to square one. You go back a hundred steps from one.

You know the worst part? You'll spend your life as a writer, curating words to explain what happened to you. And in the end, you'll fail again!!!!

6

The Suicide Note

I wondered what I would write in my last note on a moonless night. That note would be my final farewell to this world, and I would not have the chance to correct it, rewrite it, add to it, or take away from it. How will it be then? This is what followed.

"Dear ones, I know you're reading this after I'm gone, and I hope your tears are real this time. My decision to close the curtains on my act was not impulsive, and my thoughts were not clouded at all. To make it clearer for you, this is not even the first time I have died.

Every time I have been near you, I have died. The lies and forgeries, with occasional authenticity, kept me on my toes. I wondered why we can't all be real all the time. Why is it so difficult? But I was too afraid to ask because I knew you would see it as guilt and try to put it back on me. You wanted me to be fearless, and you are the reason I was afraid all the time. Even in my last moments, I wonder which of your faces is real.

I look back at my life and I can hardly recognize a happy moment. Maybe I'm just depressed, or maybe all my happiness has been taken away from me so that my craft can flourish. It makes me happy to know that I am a poet and a writer. But do I like what I write? No. It bothers me to know that the pain in my words can do no good to my readers. I'm still writing; I can't stop now. I can't dedicate my last words to those who brought me here. So I'm leaving you once and for all.

You, yes, you. You know I'm talking to you. Seeing you smile and be happy makes me happy, but at the same time my heart aches. You took care of me, you were my everything. Now I realise what a burden I was to you, although you never said so. You could have lived your life so well without me. But you were too busy taking care of me.

For me, ending my life does not throw away all your efforts. You have already made me stay longer. Now you should know that I can no longer go on like this. I can't bear the weight of all the losses, failures and betrayals of our loved ones. They have failed me and they don't even realise it.

Is there any point in arguing with people who are ignorant and wrong? Not to me. You don't waste your time with them either. Just let it all go, for it is truly my wish to see you return to glory. You are the only thing I'm proud of.

Yes, the world has tried to turn me against you, but they have failed. And they will fail in all my life cycles. My happiness means a lot to you, and I'm aware of that. If there is an afterlife, I'm sure I'll be reunited with Mummy and we'll be watching over you. Live your days to the full and then, and only then, join us. I'll be happy, I promise.

My hands are shaking, my heart is racing and I can feel life finally leaving me in peace. Don't hold on to this letter for long. You will have to let me go.

See you on the other side."

If you've made it this far, you must know that I'm fine. This letter was one of the highlights of my private collection that I wanted to share with you all. Now it's time to let go!

7

I See Death

I can see it, but I can't feel it. It's around the corner; I feel it's close. Very close. But I can only see it. I have no idea if Death can see me.

It's not machetes or daggers or even a gun. It's a tender kiss. A tiny petal. A butterfly. A hug. Is it death?

How about a dangerous face with horns? How about a club with spikes? Is it a morning star? Why does Death look so different from my imagination?

Why is it a relief? Why is it so attractive that I'm relieved every time I take a step towards it? Why does Death have such a beautiful, serene, and familiar face? Death looks like someone I've longed for. It's the peace I want and the shoulders I need. The ears for my poetry. Eyes for my tears. Death can't be a friend! Is it!?

Behind the curtains of life, death is the surprise I'm waiting for. Death is the answer to all my letters that I never sent. Death is my only friend. But my destiny won't let me be with my friends.

I don't know how to make friends. If I make one, I don't know how to keep it. There's an echo in my head. Echoes of the words I should have said out loud, but couldn't. Or maybe I didn't. And like all my relationships, death will dance to the same beats.

I can't touch death, I can't feel death.

But I can see death!!!!

8
I Can't Love You

I can't love you. I'm afraid of how this will end. It's brutal, and I've seen people lose themselves to it; I can't. Though my heart longs for you, every breath I take is a chant of your name. But I can't love you.

I can neither send you away nor walk away from your door, but I can just stand there, holding my breath with my eyes closed, trying not to hear you at all. Maybe then I can stay away from you and still be close.

Your name freezes me to the point where I can see days changing colors from the same spot. I am in love with you and so damn scared!!!!

I know my whole world is yours, but I'm too scared to let you have it. And it's not about you. It's about something I've seen happen over and over again, and no, I don't want to be in that story.

I can't love you.

9

City That Doesn't Speak

I met a hundred new faces today. Some smiled, some didn't even care that I existed. And for no good reason, I felt bad. I put aside the overwhelming duality of this city and continued my quest for some peaceful ME time.

Thousands of steps later, there I was. Right in front of the magnificent India Gate. The beauty of the monument radiated the glory of being Indian, and the Indianness of the place made me smile. I stood there for a while, letting my eyes take in the beauty of the monument and the happy faces of the children playing on the grass, completely unconcerned and unapologetic about the 'what ifs' and 'maybes' that surround the world.

I found a bench waiting for me (after passing a dozen already occupied). Waiting for this bench was justified because the view from it was exactly what I was looking for. A nearby tree opened its arms to shelter me. Lush green grass cushioned my feet, relieving me from the long walk. And for my eyes, the India Gate. Standing tall and so still. I'm pretty sure monuments don't really talk, but they do evoke conversations inside. Maybe that's why we all love them.

There was silence for a few minutes. My thoughts played in my head like the children in the garden. It got so loud that I had to close my eyes. Funny. But it works. There was silence again and I began to hear what I wanted to hear. Things I don't say out loud, things that preoccupy me even when I'm asleep. I could see them now.

Someone broke the silence. A vendor offered me something that smelled good. But I was not in the mood, so I gently declined. And then, one by one, the hawkers came. I kept refusing. Normally I get irritated by all this, but not this time. I was smiling now. But I'm still saying no.

The beauty of this place could be one of the reasons for my smile. Or maybe it was the moment of sitting with myself that did the magic for me. Luckily, I had a friend to talk to, and I could pour my heart out without being judged. I could smile without faking it. I was not forced to be funny; I was naturally great.

I stood up and took one last look at the place: the garden, the friendly bench, the caring grass, the generous tree, the smiling monument, and the loving friend. I filled my eyes with this heart-warming picture and got a drop of tears in return. I was satisfied.

I came with noise and left with the music.

10

Maybe

The unwashed dishes or the creases on the sheets. Or the dust on my shoes from the roads I walked with you. Or the scent of our last hug, or a heart drowning in the distance between us.

Or maybe the poems I wanted to tell you. Or the letter I have in my eyes for you to read out loud.

Or maybe the feeling of coming home to a hug and a promise never to let go. Or the last look before parting.

Or the unheard and unspoken confessions of love, or the dream of a life together. Or maybe just a moment of silence amidst the pounding of two chaotic hearts.

Or maybe the tears held back by uncertainty. I don't know if I can keep you for long.

Maybe I can hold on to these...

11

Insomnia

It's 3 AM. The city is in darkness and silence. No one can hear me. And here I am, sitting in a corner of my room, afraid of things I can't see. My ears are covered, trying to block out the sounds in my head. I just want to stop.

I put on my AirPods and play really loud music until my ears hurt. I couldn't move and I couldn't scream out the pain because this insomnia - this excruciating pain - is my little secret.

I never knew that something as simple as sleeping could be such an impossible task. It frustrates me to see everyone around me sleeping peacefully. I have this urge to wake them up and make them stay awake like me. To take away their peace and make them feel what I feel every night!!!

But I can't. The devil and the angel are playing games with my head. And I make sure that the angel wins and the devil consumes me inside.

Death might be worth it. It might just stop the noise and this never-ending battle I fight every day. But I'm afraid I'll have to explain my reasons to the world. And they'll never understand.

Until I decide, I just stay in a corner, look at the sun, get up, put on a mask, and go on with my act. And wait for the night to come crawling back so I can take the mask off and continue the fight.

12

Catharsis

I stare into the mirror, those big brown eyes with heavy eyelids. I try to be awake and live life somehow, although I would like to end it peacefully if at all possible. Nothing makes sense, not that I expected it to. But it's killing me and forcing me to love at the same time. I don't want to be like this!

I want to see clearly and I don't want these wet eyes anymore. I hate them. I want to look as happy as everyone around me, if possible. I want to be normal, at least for a day. I want to know what it feels like to be good, and everything I want to do makes me happy. And maybe I want to know what makes me happy right now. I don't know.

I smile, I laugh and I joke about things. Yes, I'm playful too. But every moment everything kills me and reality comes down on me and tells me that every day and every moment I spend is a façade, including me. It's a long, long act where I'm the clown with cuts and bruises under the costume. I don't want to be like that.

But I don't know if there's any other way. It's all dark now. And I'm in my room, staring into the mirror - those big brown eyes with heavy eyelids. I try to be awake and live life somehow, although I want to end it peacefully if at all possible.

13

I Set myself Free

It's time to let go of the things I've been holding on to for so long. It's time to say goodbye to the things that drag me down, fly high, hug the sky, and kiss the moon. It may take a long time, but it may be soon. But it'll be worth it, I know.

I've gotten used to these feelings and these memories. Just the thought of losing them makes me feel empty, unguarded, and vulnerable. But what's the point of all that comfort if it keeps me in a cycle of guilt, remorse, and self-pity?

I'd rather be out in the open than stuck in the dungeon we call 'the mind'. It's my time to let go and seek solace in the essence of freedom. Freedom from the vicious circle and the idea of being stuck in the same place forever.

I will talk about the things that are burning me from the inside out with the thought of letting it all out and making more space for love and gratitude within me.

In the name of God and all the energies that keep me safe and help me to learn and grow against all odds, I SET MYSELF FREE!

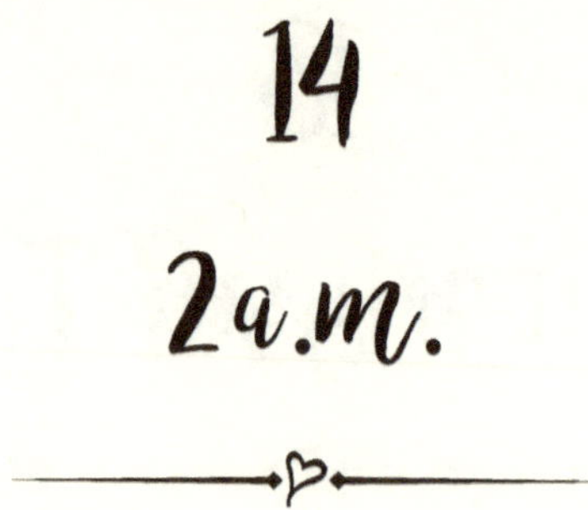

Arghhh! Here we go again!

For a year and a half, I thought the demons had left me in peace. It seems they never left. I see them standing around me, even bigger and stronger, laughing at me with their audacity.

An interesting thought: they never had faces, but now I can see them, and they all look so familiar. I have been with them for so long. No wonder they could torture me so much. They held me in their arms and offered me safety - my home. Here they are, looking at me with that pathetic grin, as if every moment I have spent with them has been an exhausting façade.

Can I fight them now? Can I chase them away or sit in their embrace? Why is it so comforting to see my demons around me after so long? Am I used to being so far away? Is this my comfort zone? Do I love living in this house of fire or do I want to break free? What's stopping me from screaming my head off and shutting them up once and for all?

What kind of magic is this? Do you know what? I will neither fight nor run. I will face them right here, right now! I am ready to face you this time. I've had enough of these 2 a.m. battles to flee the battlefield. I'm no longer afraid of you. This fight is no longer for survival; this fight is for the life I deserve. I will not back down.

Don't worry, demons; you'll see me every day.

Venue: the mind

Time: 2 a.m.

A close friend once made this for me and I have been in love with this piece of
art ever since!